AFFIRMATIONS FOR QUEER PEOPLE

AFFIRMATIONS FOR QUEER PEOPLE

100+ Positive Messages to Affirm, Empower, and Inspire

JESS VOSSETEIG

ADAMS MEDIA

New York London Toronto Sydney New Delhi

A **adams**media

Adams Media
An Imprint of Simon & Schuster, LLC
100 Technology Center Drive
Stoughton, Massachusetts 02072

First Adams Media hardcover edition
May 2024

ADAMS MEDIA and colophon
are registered trademarks of
Simon & Schuster, LLC.

Simon & Schuster: Celebrating
100 Years of Publishing in 2024

For information about special discounts
for bulk purchases, please contact
Simon & Schuster Special Sales at
1-866-506-1949 or
business@simonandschuster.com.

The Simon & Schuster Speakers Bureau
can bring authors to your live event. For
more information or to book an event,
contact the Simon & Schuster Speakers
Bureau at 1-866-248-3049 or visit our
website at www.simonspeakers.com.

Interior design, illustrations, and
hand lettering by Jess Vosseteig

Manufactured in China

10 9 8 7 6 5 4 3 2 1

Library of Congress Cataloging-in-
Publication Data
Names: Vosseteig, Jess, author. |
Adams Media (Firm), issuing body.
Title: Affirmations for Queer people /
Jess Vosseteig.
Description: Stoughton, Massachusetts:
Adams Media, [2024]
Identifiers: LCCN 2023037699 |
ISBN 9781507222263 (hc) |
ISBN 9781507222270 (ebook)
Subjects: LCSH: Sexual minorities--
Psychology. | Sexual minorities--
Mental health. | Affirmations.
Classification: LCC HQ73 .V677 2024 |
DDC 306.76--dc23/eng/20231016
LC record available at
https://lccn.loc.gov/2023037699

ISBN 978-1-5072-2226-3
ISBN 978-1-5072-2227-0 (ebook)

To my Queer community,
and to my family,
blood and chosen.
You mean the world to me.

Acknowledgments

Thank you to the entire team at Simon & Schuster for this incredible opportunity to share my art and my words with the world. I've always dreamed of making a book, and I could never have imagined that I would have the chance to create a book that aligns so perfectly with who I am as an artist and writer.

A special thanks to Tom, Kate, and Doreen—my illustration agency, Good Illustration. I am so lucky to be able to work with you all, and becoming part of your team has helped me grow so much. I appreciate all of your help and insight, always!

Thank you to my family for constantly supporting me and for everything you do for me. Mom and Dad, you gave me the tools to grow and become the person I am today, and you have always encouraged me to be myself and go after what I want. Dad, you have always helped me make smart decisions, and I wouldn't have felt so confident becoming my own business if I didn't have you as a role model. Mom, you always help me believe in myself and see my worth. You taught me to lead with love, kindness, and acceptance and now I can bring that to the world with my art. I am the luckiest kid in the world to have you both. Not every kid can say they have such unconditional love, and I am grateful for it every day. Thanks for not thinking I'm crazy for choosing to be an artist as my career. Love you!

A special thank-you to my best friend, Alyssa Wilson. I'm not kidding when I say my life would be completely different without you. You were the first person to show me you could draw on an iPad, and that literally shaped my whole career as an artist. I am so grateful to have someone to bounce my ideas off, laugh and cry with, and share our love of Queer community. You remind me that chosen family can feel just as close and be just as important. You push me to be a better artist and a better person. I'm so proud of us, and I am so beyond thankful for our friendship.

And finally, thank you to my Queer community. Your support of my art, writing, and me, keeps me excited and eager to do what I do. Thank you for reading this book and finding your own meaning in its pages. I cannot even begin to describe how much joy it brings me to think that there are Queer people who will read this book and resonate with some aspect of it. Thank you for being a place for me to explore and accept myself wholly and without judgment. I am so grateful that I have such a beautiful community to stand with me.

Keep supporting and loving each other because it makes a massive impact.

Contents

Introduction

There is so much about you that needs to be celebrated! Your individuality! Your joy! Your voice! Your strength! Your life as a Queer individual! Now with the help of affirmations, you can empower yourself and embrace all that is wonderful about you!

Affirmations are positive statements that you use to elevate your life and transform the way you think, and they are so incredibly important for members of the Queer community. After all, in a world that often tries to hide your joy and knock you down, it is critical for you to be able to validate yourself and remind yourself of your power and beauty as a Queer person.

Affirmations for Queer People contains over one hundred unique affirmations that speak directly to the joy, experiences, triumphs, and challenges faced by the Queer community. In these pages, you will find a collection of uplifting, positive, and encouraging affirmations that will help you self-reflect, celebrate your Queer identity, and find strength in yourself and your community.

Each affirmation is a reminder that you are not alone in your journey, that your voice matters, and that your existence is an act of resistance and love!

Inside you'll find motivational and inspirational affirmations like:

+ *I honor my true self as I am.*
+ *I have a loving and supportive community always by my side.*
+ *I am capable of leading a life I love.*
+ *My opinion of myself is the only one that matters.*
+ *I am a force of change.*
+ *It is not my responsibility to explain myself to others.*
+ *Happiness is my birthright as an individual.*

Wherever you are on your Queer journey, the words and images in this book will help you find strength and happiness. Let the affirmations on these pages uplift, validate, and inspire you, and remind you that being Queer is a beautiful and powerful thing!

A GUIDE to AFFIRMATIONS

You're probably excited to jump right into the affirmations and get started on your empowerment journey! But before you discover the profound effects affirmations can have on your life, you need to know a bit more about them.

Here you'll explore what affirmations are, as well as their significance. You'll see why affirmations are such compelling tools for personal growth and empowerment—especially for Queer individuals—and you'll discover how affirmations can help you release internalized shame and change your perspective on life. With affirmations by your side, you'll be able to navigate the complexities of your identity and reclaim your power in a world that often seeks to marginalize and silence you.

Remember, this book is not just a passive reading experience. It is an invitation for you to actively engage with these affirmations and integrate them into your daily life. By consistently practicing affirmations, you can harness their strength and create positive changes in your mindset and life! Embrace the journey of self-discovery, self-acceptance, and self-empowerment that awaits you.

What Are Affirmations?

Sure, you may be wondering how a few words and pictures in a book can change your life—but believe it! That is just how powerful affirmations can be. Affirmations are short, positive statements that, when repeated over and over to yourself, can actually alter your way of thinking and change the way you feel about yourself. Affirmations are meant to counteract and challenge your negative thoughts. By stopping the negativity in its tracks and replacing it with uplifting, peaceful, and joyous thoughts, you are rewriting the negative thoughts and shame that may be plaguing you and transforming your life in the process. Affirmations serve as reminders of your worth and your unique identities, and help you embrace who you truly are.

Affirmations have actually been used for thousands of years. The ancient Hindus and Buddhists used mantras (repeated words or phrases) as part of meditation and as a way to quiet the mind. Affirmations are similar to mantras because you can repeat them for a more positive state of mind. During the nineteenth century, the use of affirmations became popular as people discovered the power of positive thinking. Then, in the twentieth century, the practice of affirmations exploded as people around the world began using affirmations to improve their lives.

Why Affirmations Are Important for Queer People

Affirmations are not only important because they help you grow a positive mindset, boost your self-confidence, and support your personal growth; they can also help you respond to threats. Affirmations allow you to feel more resilient and adaptive to your environment and any challenges that you might face; as Queer people, having these abilities is crucial. Having the tools to feel confident and happy, and create the life you deserve is incredibly powerful for Queer people. We will always deal with negativity and discrimination, but if you have a tool belt of positive affirmations to counteract that negativity, you can be unstoppable! No one can teach you to be yourself, so it's crucial that you give yourself the support and encouragement that you deserve as a Queer individual. You can always rely on yourself, and having positive and affirming phrases to come back to when things get tough can be very helpful and comforting.

Affirmations for Queer People can help provide a safe space for self-exploration and self-expression. The affirmations in this book address a wide range of unique challenges you might face as a Queer person.

RELEASING SHAME

As a Queer person, you have no doubt been exposed to shame and negativity from others. In order to be able to create belonging with our community, you must first be able to release and unlearn this internalized shame. Using affirmations can help you talk positively to yourself and encourage yourself, making you a more empowered and confident individual. By doing this, you create a ripple effect that inspires other Queer people to find self-love too!

It is important for Queer individuals to be intentional with unlearning the shame and stigmas placed upon them because that is exactly what society does not want. The patriarchal and heteronormative society we live in is afraid of anything outside of those norms, so being able to unlearn the shame that comes with being different is going to be a way to create change. Queer people have been silenced throughout history, and the only way for us to make change in the world is to use our voices and be seen and heard.

Loving yourself despite the hatred of others is such an effective way to counteract discrimination. If everyone who is Queer could be proud of that fact, we could all come together in self-love and have the capacity to fight back against hate. By being Queer and proud—and arming yourself with the right mental tools like affirmations to exist in a world that tries to tear you down—you are claiming your power back.

EXAMINING INTERSECTIONALITY

The affirmations in this book will also help you appreciate and embrace the intersectionality in the Queer community. *Intersectionality* is a term coined by the leading scholar of critical race theory and activist Kimberlé Crenshaw. It is a lens through which you can examine how everyone has intersecting parts of their identities that affect each other. For example, the experiences of Queer individuals intersect with other aspects of their identities, such as race, ethnicity, socioeconomic status, disability, and more. Intersectionality acknowledges that these different dimensions of identity can shape a person's lived experiences and the challenges they face.

The Queer community is very diverse and encompasses people from various backgrounds, each with their own unique set of struggles and triumphs. By recognizing and celebrating the diversity within the community, the affirmations in this book can help everyone feel seen, validated, and empowered to embrace their multiple identities. The affirmations you will read aim to address a wide range of challenges that Queer individuals might face. Hopefully you can see yourself in some of the affirmations in this book and affirm yourself in all your overlapping identities. It is through this inclusivity that we can foster a sense of belonging and unity within the Queer community.

EFFECTING CHANGE

Affirmations have the power not only to transform *your* individual life but also to shape the collective future for *all* Queer people! When you use affirmations, you are actively challenging societal norms and narratives that perpetuate discrimination and inequality. By affirming your worth, celebrating your identities, and embracing your authentic self, you become a catalyst for change in your communities and beyond.

Additionally, affirmations can create a sense of solidarity within the Queer community. By embracing our diverse identities and intersectional experiences, we build a foundation of empathy, understanding, and support. Affirmations that acknowledge the struggles and triumphs of different individuals can create a sense of belonging and unity. When we uplift and empower each other through affirmations, we strengthen the collective Queer community and are more capable of overcoming adversity together.

Affirmations are not just a personal practice but a force for societal transformation. They empower us to create change for ourselves and future generations, challenge oppressive systems, and build a more inclusive and accepting world for all Queer individuals. Through affirmations, you can shape a future where every person is celebrated, valued, and able to live their truth without fear or discrimination.

✦ How to Use Affirmations ✦

There are many ways to use affirmations to elevate your life. You can start the day every morning by saying an affirmation to yourself, you can say them during a designated meditation or quiet time, or you can use them when you're in moments of distress to help you get through. The important thing is to repeat the affirmation to yourself until it becomes your dominant thought. When you find yourself in a spiral of negative thoughts or emotions, look for an affirmation in this book that speaks to you, and repeat it until you can't think of anything else except the words you are saying. There is power in being intentional with your thoughts and actions. Repeating these uplifting statements will make seeing the positive side of life a habit that sticks in your brain. Eventually it will become second nature for your brain to replace negative thoughts with positive ones!

As simple as it sounds, repeating an affirmation to help your mindset might be tough at first. If you are dealing with a lot of internalized shame, personal doubts, or societal stigmas, using affirmations might be really difficult for you, which is completely okay! Learning to unlearn certain thoughts and feelings that society has imposed upon you will be difficult, but it's important to be patient with yourself and try to be open. Like anything new, practice is all it takes.

✦ Choosing Affirmations ✦

This book is designed for you to have access to all the affirmations in one place. Feel free to read through them sequentially from beginning to end or jump around and read whatever catches your eye! If reading through all of them at once isn't for you, try flipping through and letting the affirmations speak to you. You just might find the perfect affirmation for however you are feeling. Please note that affirmations can be very personal, and this book is meant to be as inclusive as possible—however, this means that not all of the affirmations will apply to you! For example, if you don't personally identify as transgender and you come across affirmations that speak to that specific part of the community, feel free to share it with a trans person in your life!

This book is for you to celebrate and be comfortable in your Queer identity, so mark it up, bookmark your favorite affirmations, even rip out the pages to take with you or hang up if you want. There are some specific suggestions for how you can use certain affirmations, but do whatever feels right for you! Try writing some of your favorite ones out on sticky notes and putting them around your house, or keep a journal of some of the affirmations that speak to you and jot down how you can apply them in your personal life. Whatever you decide to do with the affirmations, the point of this book is to be your safe space!

✦ Moving Forward ✦

Now that you are familiar with what affirmations are, how they work, and how they can work for you as a Queer person, remember that these affirmations have the power to transform your mindset and empower you on your journey. By embracing positive self-talk and affirming your worth, you can create profound change within yourself and your community. As you read through the affirmations in this book, let them serve as reminders of your strength, your uniqueness, and your ability to create a more inclusive and affirming world. Remember to go into the rest of this book with an open and patient mind, and hopefully you will find plenty of affirmations that fit right in with your journey as a Queer individual!

AFFIRMATIONS

Are you ready to discover the power of positive affirmations? Remember, these words are here to remind you of your worth, your strength, and your limitless potential as a Queer person. The following pages create a safe space where you can be unapologetically *you*.

Here you will find more than one hundred affirmations, each one carefully crafted to speak directly to the Queer experience. Each affirmation comes with a bite-sized blurb that'll give you inspiration and guidance on how to use it. Feel free to try out what is suggested or find your own ways to use each affirmation most effectively for your journey. There is no wrong way to read or use any of these affirmations! To make these affirmations really come to life for you, there are illustrations scattered throughout the following pages. These illustrations are meant to give you a visual depiction of the affirmations and to capture Queer joy and empowerment. The hope is that you can feel seen in this artwork and let it fill you with positivity and validation!

Feel free to spread the joy of these affirmations and share them with your chosen family or Queer community so we can all feel empowered and valid in our identities! By sharing these inspiring words, you can create a ripple effect of positivity and acceptance in your community. Embrace these affirmations because they are here to fuel your courage and passion as you live your most authentic Queer life!

Being fluid is beautiful.

Know that your journey is not confined to fixed definitions. Celebrate the ever-changing and evolving aspects of yourself! Embrace the freedom of fluidity, allowing yourself to explore and express all the nuances of your identity. Repeat this affirmation with pride, knowing that being fluid is a powerful and beautiful aspect of your unique Queer self.

I have a loving and supportive community always by my side.

Queer individuals are part of a beautiful, diverse, and expansive community that offers love and support. Use this affirmation to remind yourself that you are never alone. Let the love and support of the Queer community lift you up when others bring you down. Say it before bed or in the morning to start your day with love and support!

I deserve a full and happy life.

Your sexual orientation or gender identity should never be a barrier to living a life of joy and purpose. Embrace this reminder to prioritize self-care, pursue your passions, and surround yourself with positive influences that uplift and support you! You deserve nothing less than a life that is vibrant and overflowing with happiness.

My community supports me when others don't.

In times when you face rejection or a lack of understanding from others, the Queer community can always offer unwavering support. Even when faced with adversity, you are not alone. Your community becomes your chosen family who can provide you with love, strength, and unconditional acceptance. Lean on this affirmation as a source of strength, knowing that there are people who genuinely understand and appreciate you for who you are.

I accept myself as I am at this moment.

With so many societal pressures and expectations upon you, it is critical to wholeheartedly accept yourself. If you can accept your unique journey, you can celebrate your experiences and identities without judgment. This is your daily reminder to love yourself unconditionally as you are. You don't have to wait to give yourself love and acceptance. Try saying this affirmation when you wake up to start your day right.

I am always evolving into who I want to be.

Let's celebrate the continuous growth and self-discovery that we face as Queer people! Our journey is ever-changing, and we have the power to shape our identities. We can embrace the fluidity of our identities while exploring and honoring the beautiful process of becoming who we truly want to be. Use this affirmation as a reminder of your ability to grow and transform!

My identity is for me and no other.

Your self-expression, labels, and experiences are valid and should not be influenced by external expectations or judgments. Your identity reflects who you are, and you have the power to define it for yourself. Embrace this affirmation as a powerful declaration that your identity is yours to embrace, celebrate, and explore without seeking validation or approval from others.

I have the ability to choose my family.

Queer people often do not find acceptance within their biological families. If your biological family rejects you or refuses to give you the support you need, you have the ability to choose your own family. You have the freedom to build your own family with your friends or other members of the Queer community. Use this affirmation as a reminder that you can create meaningful connections and build relationships that uplift and celebrate your unique identities.

I am constantly expanding my ideas about gender and sexuality.

Sometimes we need to remind ourselves to embrace curiosity, open-mindedness, and a willingness to learn as we challenge societal norms and expand our understanding of diverse identities. By embracing this affirmation, you give yourself permission to explore and celebrate the spectrum of gender and sexuality. Let it inspire you to continue seeking knowledge and embrace a more inclusive and expansive world!

I don't have to have "experience" to be valid in my Queerness.

Queerness is not defined by specific experiences or milestones. Your Queerness is valid simply because it is a part of who you are. Free yourself from the pressure of expectations and allow yourself to define your Queerness on your own terms! Use this affirmation as a mantra whenever you feel self-doubt about your Queer experiences.

My period doesn't make me any less valid as a man.

Menstruation is not exclusive to women—trans men and nonbinary people also menstruate! As a Queer person, it's essential to recognize that gender and sex are two separate ideas that don't always align. Use this affirmation to affirm your masculinity and reject societal stereotypes. Try putting this affirmation on your menstrual products so you have a reminder that your identity as a man is valid and not diminished by menstruation.

I deserve access to healthcare.

Feel empowered to demand equal access to healthcare services that address your unique needs and support your overall well-being! Everyone deserves comprehensive and inclusive healthcare services, but sadly a lot of Queer people do not get the care they need. Repeat this affirmation to assert your rights and advocate for yourself when seeking medical care. Use it as a reminder that your health and well-being matter, and you deserve to receive respectful, affirming, and competent healthcare!

I AM A FIERCE AND EMPOWERED INDIVIDUAL!

I deserve the love I want.

Queer love knows no bounds, and you deserve to love whoever and however you want! Queer people are often shamed for who they love, but this is a reminder that you deserve any type of love you desire. Embrace this affirmation and watch as you attract the love you want into your life.

I am allowed to change my identity.

You are allowed to change your identity at any time! Be empowered to explore, question, and redefine who you are at any point in your life. There is a lot of self-exploration that comes with being Queer, and sometimes that means your labels or identity will grow and change with you. Give yourself permission to shed old labels, adopt new ones, and honor your ever-evolving identity! Say this affirmation whenever you feel doubt about changing your mind on your labels.

I can come out whenever it feels right to me.

Coming out is such an intense and liberating experience, but it can also be very nerve-wracking and overwhelming. Don't let anyone pressure you into a certain timeline or coming-out experience. You have the power to come out on your own terms and only when you feel ready!

I don't have to come out in a particular way.

Your coming-out journey is as unique as you are! No one will ever have the exact same experience coming out, so don't feel stressed about doing it in a certain way. Your truth is valid no matter how you choose to share it with others! Remind yourself of this affirmation if you are feeling anxious about coming out to anyone.

I AM QUEER ENOUGH.

I love being able to choose who I love.

Love is not confined by gender, sexuality, or societal expectations. Allow this affirmation to guide you toward the realization that your heart knows no limits when it comes to love. People who identify as bisexual/pansexual/polyamorous and anyone else this resonates with can use this affirmation to affirm their right to choose who they love!

I love being a part of a history full of strength.

Recognize and celebrate the rich history of resilience, courage, and strength within the Queer community. Remember all of the trailblazers who came before you that paved the way for progress. Regardless of how you identify, you can honor the collective history of the Queer community and encourage yourself to feel proud and empowered to be a part of it! Be inspired to contribute to the ongoing legacy of strength, and continue advocating for a more inclusive and accepting world.

My past does not define me.

Your history does not define you as a Queer individual. You may have faced many challenges, traumas, and experiences as a Queer person growing up, but none of those experiences define who you are. Embrace the limitless potential of your future, and allow yourself to break free from any past limitations. Write this affirmation somewhere you will see it often to have a constant reminder that your past doesn't define you.

I don't have to use a label to define myself.

In a world that constantly tries to categorize and label everything, this is a reminder that your identity cannot be confined to a box. Embrace the freedom to exist authentically and unapologetically as you are! You are not defined by labels, and if you don't want to use a label to identify yourself, you don't have to! Remember that your identity is boundless and can transcend societal expectations.

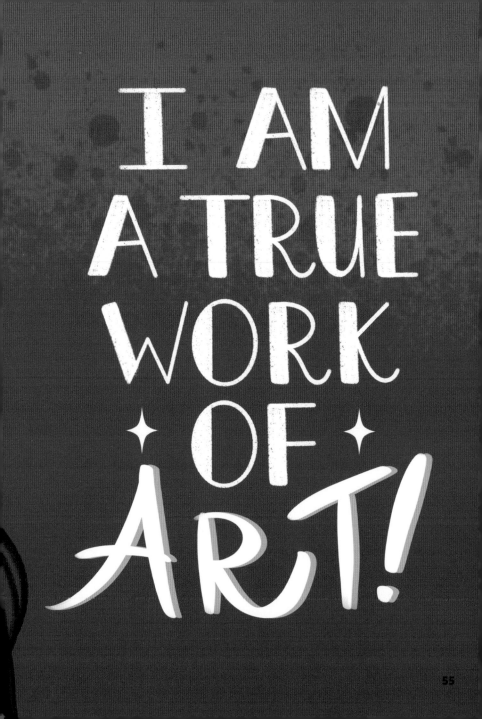

I AM A TRUE WORK OF ✦ OF ✦ ART!

I choose what my identity means to me.

In a world that often tries to define you, you have the power to shape and define your own identity. Your identity is a personal and unique journey, and only you have the authority to determine what it means to you. Say this affirmation to yourself whenever you question the validity of whatever identities you claim!

My opinion of myself is the only one that matters.

Your self-worth is not determined by the opinions of others. A lot of people have opinions on how Queer people live their lives, but those opinions do not define you. Embrace the power of self-validation, celebrating your uniqueness and your personal journey. Prioritize how you think of yourself. Your opinion of yourself is the only one that truly matters at the end of the day!

I am capable of leading a life I love.

We have the power and ability to shape our own lives into whatever makes us happy. As Queer people, we are often told that our lives will be difficult and unfulfilling. But you have the power to have a life that aligns with your true self and is filled with joy! Embrace the idea that you are capable of creating a life filled with love, purpose, and happiness.

I am always learning new things about myself.

As a Queer individual, you can recognize that your identity and experiences are not fixed. Stay open-minded, curious, and open to the knowledge that comes with self-exploration. Self-reflection is going to be a constant in your life as a Queer person, so let this affirmation remind you that self-discovery is a beautiful, lifelong process!

+ I AM +
worthy
OF
healthy
AND
fulfilling
RELATIONSHIPS

I don't have to explain myself to anyone.

You don't owe anyone an explanation for your identity, your choices, or your existence! Your journey is valid and deserving of respect, regardless of whether others understand or accept it. Let this affirmation give you the confidence to live authentically, without needing any validation or approval from anyone else.

I am not a burden.

A lot of Queer people might internalize the discrimination and lack of acceptance from society, making them feel like a burden to others. You can challenge and reject those internalized negative beliefs because they are not your reality! Embrace your authentic self, knowing that your presence is a gift! You are worthy of love, compassion, and support, just as you are.

There is no "correct" way to transition.

In the journey of transitioning, it's important to remember that there is no single correct way to navigate this process. Embrace the freedom to define what transitioning means to you. Whether it involves medical interventions, social changes, or personal growth, your transition is yours to define. Use this affirmation when you are feeling pressured from society to transition in a specific way.

I can change my pronouns anytime I want.

One of the beautiful aspects of Queer identity is the fluidity and ability to change and explore what you identify with. You have the power to define and express your gender in whatever ways you want. This affirmation reminds you that you can always change what pronouns you use for yourself. Choosing what pronouns feel right for you might be a process, and you have the freedom to explore that!

I
celebrate
the
beautiful
spectrum
of the
Queer
community.

67

I am enough as I am.

In a world that is constantly trying to diminish Queer people, know that you are enough just as you are! You don't need to meet any unrealistic societal expectations or meet anyone's standards. Embrace who you are in this current moment. Put this affirmation on your mirror to remind yourself every day that you are enough just as you are!

I am powerful and strong.

It takes a lot of strength to be your authentic self in a world that doesn't always understand. Despite facing societal challenges and prejudices, you possess a resilience that empowers you to overcome any obstacle. Let this affirmation be a constant reminder of your power, both individually and as part of the Queer community. You are powerful and strong, and your presence in the world makes a difference.

I deserve to feel safe and stable.

You have an inherent right as a Queer person to feel safe and stable in all aspects of your life. You deserve to exist in spaces where you feel respected, valued, and protected. Embrace the belief that you are deserving of a life free from discrimination, prejudice, and harm. Surround yourself with supportive and inclusive communities that prioritize your well-being and provide the safety and stability you deserve. Remember this affirmation in times of stress or uncertainty.

I don't have to fit anyone's expectations.

Queer people are constantly forced to fit other people's expectations of what we are "supposed to" look like, act like, and so on. Use this affirmation as a reminder that you don't have to fit into stereotypes or adhere to anyone's ideas about you. Don't let other people's expectations of you get you down!

It's okay to be confused about my sexuality/ gender.

Gender and sexuality are such vast and fluid concepts that it can be really difficult to pin down what might feel right for you. Queerness is a journey, and you can allow yourself time and space to figure it out! It's okay to not know everything right now. Let this affirmation be a reminder when you feel pressured to figure it all out.

I won't allow anyone to have power over me.

You are the owner of your life. People often try to impose their own ideas onto others, but remember that you get to define your worth in this world. No one has power over you unless you give it to them. You are valid as you are—and no one can take that away from you!

I unapologetically embrace my unique journey.

Your path is unlike anyone else's! By embracing your unique journey, you allow yourself to be who you are without limitation and without comparison. Let this be a reminder to embrace your experiences, and find strength in the knowledge that your journey is proof of your strength and unique self.

Celebrating my Queerness is an act of self-love and empowerment.

Embrace your Queerness and love yourself! By celebrating your unique identity, you affirm your authentic self. By celebrating your Queerness, you allow others to feel like they can celebrate their Queerness too! Unapologetically embrace and celebrate your Queerness, knowing that it is an expression of love, resilience, and self-acceptance.

I EMBRACE THE *freedom* TO EXIST *beyond* THE BINARY.

I honor my true self as I am.

It is a powerful act of self-acceptance and self-respect to honor your true self. By embracing your authentic identity, you celebrate the unique combination of experiences, emotions, and qualities that make you who you are. Make sure to prioritize your own well-being and stay true to your values, desires, and dreams.

I am resilient.

Celebrate the collective strength that the Queer community can give you. Queer people go through so many challenges in life, and this is your reminder that you are strong and resilient in the face of adversity. The Queer community will always be at your side to help you. Repeat this affirmation when you are faced with challenges in your life.

I am capable of overcoming any challenges that come my way.

Queer individuals often face challenges and adversity from others. Know that you can navigate any challenge that comes your way and come out of it a stronger and more capable person. You have already overcome so much; keep using your strength to guide you through. You are more than capable of facing anything that comes your way.

I rise above discrimination and adversity.

Be empowered to rise above any biases or prejudice from others. Queer people are constantly dealing with discrimination, but know that you are capable of not letting negativity get to you! By rising above adversity, you not only reclaim your power, but you also help others feel capable of doing the same.

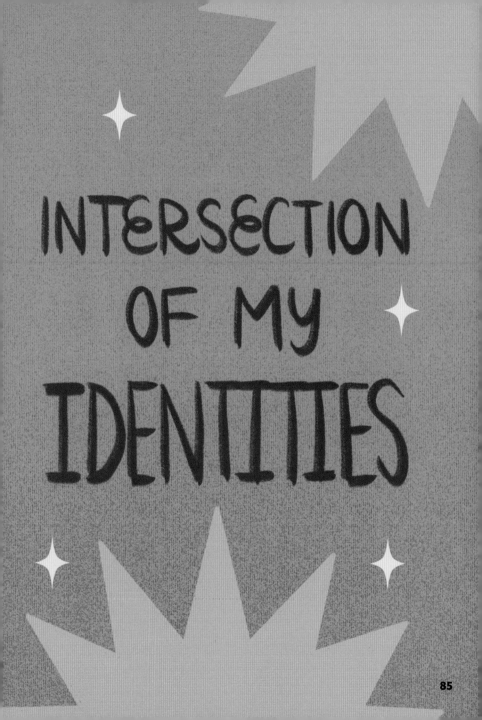

INTERSECTION OF MY IDENTITIES

I embrace the beauty of diverse experiences.

The Queer community is full of unique stories, journeys, and perspectives that make us who we are! We need to celebrate the richness that comes from embracing our differences. No one's experiences or stories are the same, which is what makes the Queer community so beautiful. By appreciating and valuing diverse experiences, we create a space where everyone feels seen, heard, and loved.

Change is possible.

At times it can be difficult to feel hopeful about progress for Queer rights, but change is possible! You have the ability to help your community come together and make waves in the world. We are stronger when we unite, and this is your reminder that change is possible when we work together!

I contribute to the dismantling of oppressive systems.

Being Queer is, in itself, an act of resistance to oppressive systems! Every act of resistance to the status quo contributes to a brighter and more inclusive future. Together we are a powerful force that refuses to be silenced or marginalized! Keep being your true self, speaking out, and breaking barriers.

I surround myself with love and support.

Surround yourself with love and support and create a safe space for yourself. Cultivate a chosen family of allies who celebrate your Queerness and offer encouragement and acceptance. You deserve a support system that radiates positivity. Allow yourself to be open to receiving the love and support you deserve as your authentic self.

I LOVE IN ALL

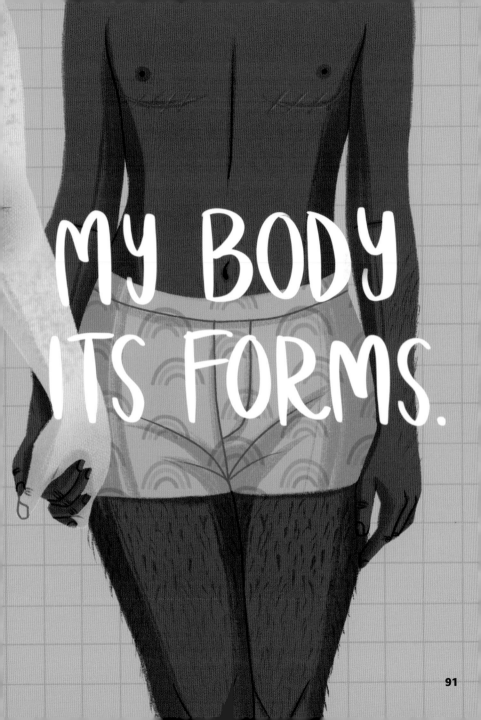

MY BODY
ITS FORMS.

It is not my responsibility to explain myself to others.

You are not obligated to justify or explain your Queer identity to anyone. Your truth and self-expression are valid on their own, independent of others' understanding or acceptance. Embrace the freedom of simply being who you are, without the burden of conforming to their expectations. Your Queerness is yours to own and celebrate, unapologetically. Live authentically, and use this affirmation as a reminder that you owe no explanations or apologies for embracing your true self.

I am not obligated to teach anyone how to respect me.

It is not your responsibility to enlighten or change the minds of those who fail to acknowledge or understand your worth. Instead, focus on valuing and respecting yourself, and surround yourself with others who already embrace and celebrate your authentic self. Your energy is better invested in cultivating spaces of love and acceptance, where your Queerness is celebrated without question or expectation. Remember, your self-worth does not depend on the validation or understanding of others.

I am a force of change.

By embracing your Queerness and advocating for equality and acceptance, you can create change. Your voice, actions, and presence have the potential to challenge societal norms, break down barriers, and inspire others to stand up for their own rights. Embrace your role as a force of change, knowing that your efforts contribute to a more inclusive and accepting world for all Queer individuals. Together, we can create a future where everyone can live authentically and without fear.

I am capable of achieving greatness.

Queer people are often worried that their identity might get in the way of their ability to achieve the things they want in life. Your identity does not limit your potential—instead, it adds depth and richness to your journey. Believe in yourself and your abilities because you have the power to accomplish amazing things. You are capable of achieving greatness in every aspect of your life, making a lasting impact on the world around you.

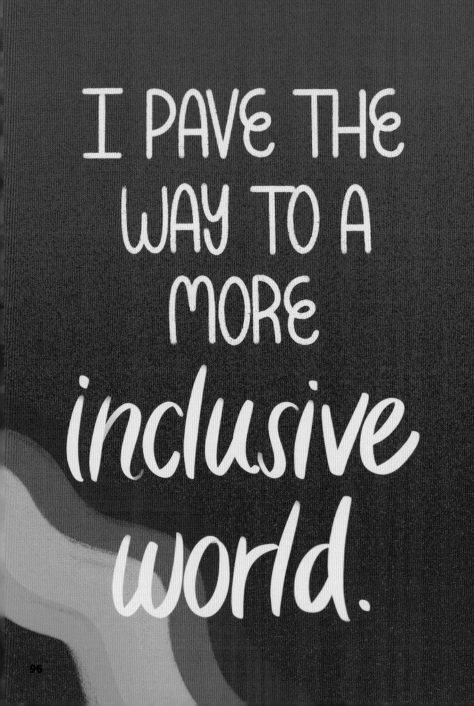

I PAVE THE WAY TO A MORE inclusive world.

My strength has brought me this far.

Reflect on the resilience and courage that you have inside you. Acknowledge the battles you've fought and the progress you've made, recognizing that your strength is a testament to your spirit. Your strength is an enduring source of inspiration, reminding you of the incredible heights you can reach as you continue to navigate your unique journey. Remember this affirmation when you feel discouraged.

I extend the love and respect I deserve to myself.

As a Queer individual, it's important to not allow other people to be your only source of support and love—you are the most important person in your life. By extending the love and respect you deserve to yourself, you create a solid foundation for personal growth and well-being. Celebrate your worth, honor your boundaries, and prioritize your own happiness.

I face challenges with courage and dignity.

As a Queer individual, you have demonstrated immense resilience in navigating obstacles in your life. Every Queer person will inevitably face challenges on their path of self-discovery, but the mindset you have about them is what matters. Remember: You possess the strength and determination to face any challenge with courage and dignity, and you can emerge stronger on the other side.

Every challenge I face is an opportunity for growth.

You are going to face challenges constantly throughout life, but look at them as a way to bring new change and growth. As a Queer person, you have the ability to take on challenges and allow them to be catalysts for personal growth and self-discovery. Try reframing difficulties as stepping stones on your journey. Embrace every challenge as a way to create a brighter future for yourself!

I
STAND
CONFIDENTLY
IN MY
TRUTH!

I bring a new perspective to the world.

Your unique experiences as a Queer individual challenge societal norms and expand the boundaries of acceptance and inclusivity. Your existence breaks down barriers and paves the way for a more inclusive future. Embrace the power of your voice and the impact it has on shaping a more accepting and understanding world. Embrace your role as a trailblazer, and know that your perspective is an essential part of the collective narrative of progress and change.

I can find support in shared experiences with others.

You can find strength and solace by connecting with others who have similar paths to yours. By recognizing and embracing shared experiences, you create a sense of belonging and understanding. It can be a powerful feeling to be able to relate to so many others in the Queer community. Through these connections, you can find validation, empathy, and resilience, and create bonds that remind you that you are never alone on your Queer journey.

I pave the way for others who come after me.

By embracing your authentic self and living your truth, you become a beacon of hope and inspiration for other Queer people. You being you makes you a trailblazer and someone that others can look to as an example. Your visibility and resilience inspire others to embrace their identities, dream bigger, and live authentically. Together, we can build a world where future generations can thrive and be celebrated for who they are.

I can allow myself to feel joy.

Being Queer comes with challenges and oftentimes fear, but by allowing yourself to feel joy, you reclaim your right to celebrate every aspect of your identity and existence. Queer joy is an act of resistance and self-love! Let it radiate from within you and inspire others to find their own happiness while navigating a world that tries to push down Queer joy. Repeat this affirmation to yourself when you have a hard time letting go and enjoying the moment.

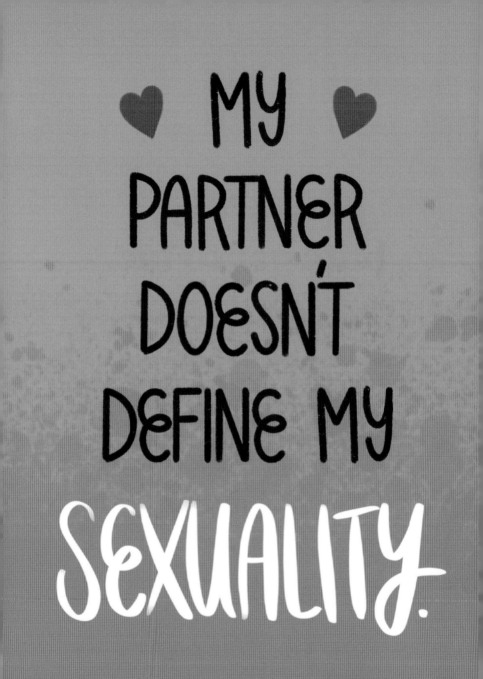

MY PARTNER DOESN'T DEFINE MY SEXUALITY.

I won't let hate get to me.

As a Queer individual, you have probably faced hate and discrimination along your journey. But in the face of such negativity, you stand tall, unwavering in your authenticity. Refuse to let negativity affect your self-worth. Arm yourself with self-love and acceptance, and remember that people's bigotry does not define you. Keep forging ahead, unyielding and unapologetic, knowing that you are deserving of respect and love, and that hate cannot break you.

I appreciate my body's strength and uniqueness.

Your body carries you through a world that often seeks to undermine and invalidate it. Let go of societal expectations and standards, and instead, celebrate the magnificence of your body just as it is. Cherish your body, nurture it, and let it be a source of pride and gratitude. Embrace the power and beauty of your unique body because it allows you to overcome obstacles and shine authentically in the world.

My worth is not defined by societal standards.

In a world that tries to confine you to societal standards, rise above and claim your worth! Your value cannot be defined by narrow expectations or conforming to norms. Let this affirmation be a reminder that you are inherently valuable—deserving of love, respect, and self-acceptance. Embrace your authentic self and reject limitations. Repeat this affirmation as a reminder of your inherent worth and the power of being authentically you.

I release any shame I've internalized.

You have the power to release any shame you might feel about your identity or your journey as a Queer person. Society often places shame on Queer people, but if you can acknowledge and release any shame you might have internalized, you create space for self-acceptance, love, and growth. Repeat this affirmation on your journey toward self-love and liberation. You deserve to live authentically, without the weight of shame.

my VOICE MATTERS!

I celebrate every milestone in my Queer journey.

Each step forward, no matter how small, is important for your journey of growth. Embrace the victories, both big and small, and honor the progress you've made along your Queer journey. Whether it's coming out, getting gender-affirming procedures, having your first Queer crush, or changing your pronouns, take a moment to acknowledge and celebrate these milestones! Let this affirmation be a reminder to find joy in every part of your Queer journey.

Happiness is my birthright as an individual.

Society may try to undermine your feelings and your happiness, but remember that everyone on this earth deserves to be happy. Claim your happiness and feel Queer joy despite any obstacle. Embrace your authenticity and let it fuel your happiness! You deserve to feel good and live with joy as a Queer individual.

I uplift and support my Queer siblings.

You hold the power to uplift and support our community, and it is a crucial responsibility. In a world that often tries to divide us, our solidarity becomes a powerful force for change. By uplifting and supporting one another, we create a safe and caring environment where we can all thrive. Do your best to lift up your Queer family, and they will do the same for you.

I spread compassion and acceptance wherever I go.

Because you understand what it feels like to not be accepted, you spread positivity and acceptance to others around you. Your presence, words, and actions can make other people feel accepted and loved. Embrace this power wherever you go, and know you can be a beacon of hope for others. Even when it might be difficult, remember to spread the love you want to receive.

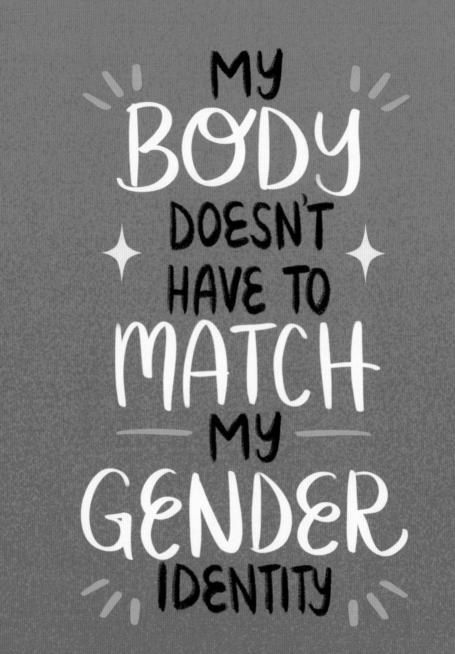

MY BODY DOESN'T HAVE TO MATCH MY GENDER IDENTITY

I release the weight of societal expectations.

As a Queer individual, you may have felt the burden of conforming to norms that do not align with your true self. By releasing these expectations, you reclaim your power and pave the way for self-discovery and self-acceptance. Trust in your own path and journey, knowing that your worth is not defined by external standards. Embrace the freedom that comes with living life on your own terms and watch your life flourish.

I have the right to exist as a Queer person.

Your identity is valid, and your presence in this world is valuable and necessary. No one has the power to diminish your worth or deny your existence. Stand tall, unapologetic and proud of who you are. Embrace the truth that your existence as a Queer person is a beautiful and essential part of our diverse world. Repeat this affirmation as a reminder of your inherent right to exist, be seen, and be celebrated!

I validate my own experiences.

Your lived experiences are valid and meaningful, and you can always trust yourself to know this is true. By validating your own experiences, you reclaim your voice and affirm the importance of your story. Use this as a reminder that your experiences matter and deserve to be acknowledged and honored, both by yourself and by others.

I replace self-doubt with self-compassion.

In moments of self-doubt, you have the power to shift your mindset and replace it with compassion. Instead of allowing doubt to consume you, choose to be gentle and kind to yourself. As a Queer person, you might doubt your feelings at times, but it is important to be compassionate and patient with yourself! Embrace self-compassion as a powerful tool to counteract negative thoughts and beliefs.

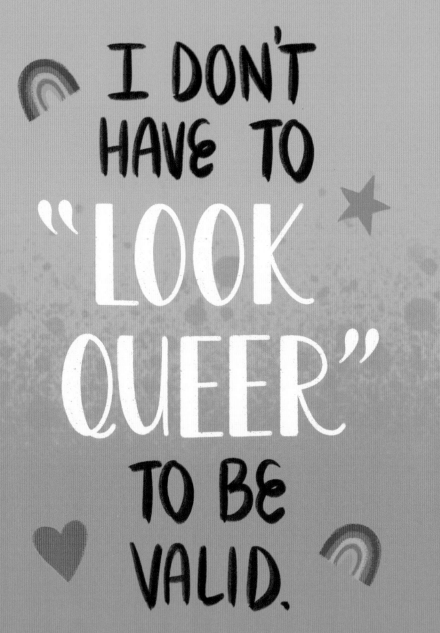

I DON'T HAVE TO "LOOK QUEER" TO BE VALID.

I embrace the power of mindfulness.

As a Queer individual, mindfulness can be an empowering practice to help you navigate the complexities of your journey. By being fully present in each moment, you gain a heightened sense of self-awareness, acceptance, and compassion. Embrace mindfulness as a tool to ground yourself, to find solace in the present, and to navigate challenges with clarity and peace.

I allow
the energy
of the universe
to flow
through me.

Allow yourself to be open to the positive
energy that surrounds you, connecting
with the world in a way that feels authentic
and empowering. Repeat this affirmation
as a reminder to stay grounded and
connected, drawing upon the energy of
the universe to support and guide you on
your journey. Let the positive energy flow
through you, empowering you to create
a life that aligns with your authentic self.

I respect all spiritual paths and everyone's Queer journey.

Respect and acceptance are at the center of the Queer community. Recognize that each person's Queer journey is deeply personal and deserves validation. By respecting and honoring different spiritual beliefs, we foster a sense of unity and create a safe space for all Queer individuals. Repeat this affirmation as a reminder to approach others with an open heart and mind, embracing the beauty of our collective experiences.

I am supported and guided by a higher power.

Know that you are supported by a higher power, whatever that may mean to you. Trust in the divine energy that flows through your life, providing strength and encouragement on your journey. Embrace the belief that you are never alone because you are held and supported by a power greater than yourself. If you personally don't believe in any higher power, feel free to share this affirmation with someone in your life who does!

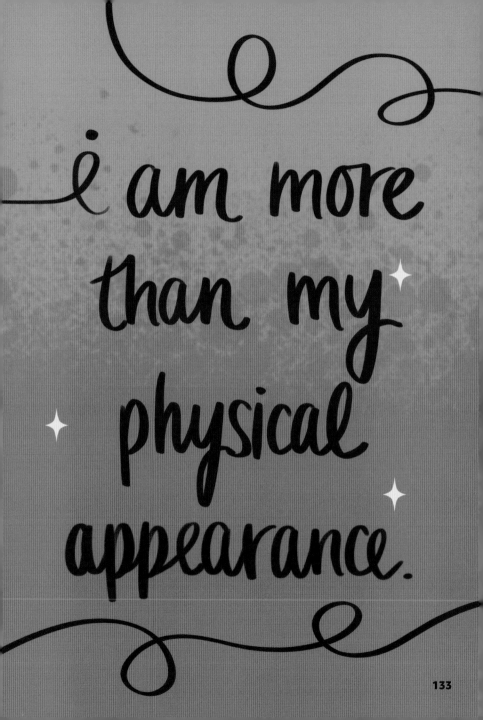

i am more than my physical appearance.

I am on a healing journey.

As a Queer person, you are constantly healing from societal pressures and norms. Being a Queer person gives you the ability to stay open-minded about life, which can help you heal from past traumas or wounds. Repeat this affirmation when you need a reminder that life is a process, and healing is part of your journey.

I allow myself time and space to process past traumas.

Give yourself permission to let go of any lingering pain that might be in your heart. Being Queer often comes with its challenges, but by recognizing and allowing yourself the time and space to process those challenges, you can overcome them. Seek support from your community, and be patient with yourself as you heal.

I have the capacity to heal and survive.

Throughout history, the Queer community has shown that we are strong and can overcome adversity. You also possess this power as a Queer person, and you are never alone. Embrace your ability to not only heal and survive, but to thrive and live your life to the fullest—because it is possible.

I will find the support and resources I need.

If you can recognize that you need or want help and support, you will be able to find it. The Queer community is always standing behind you, ready to help you on your journey. Seek out networks, communities, and organizations that can be helpful to you! You can also find some resources at the end of this book. Remind yourself that you can find support.

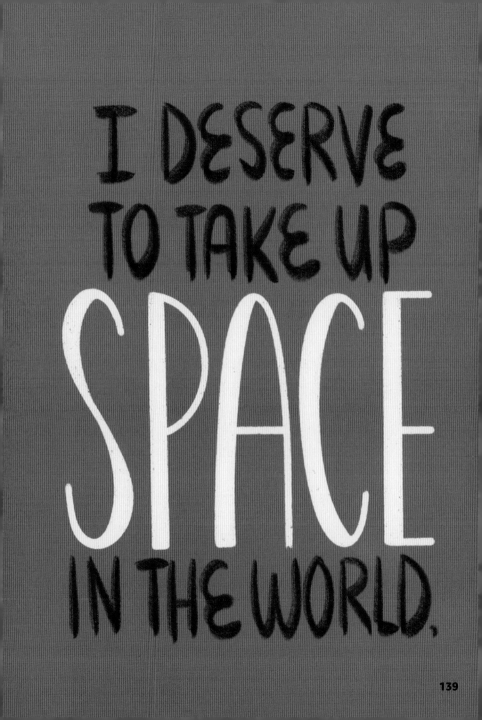

I DESERVE TO TAKE UP SPACE IN THE WORLD.

I am not defined by the rejection I've experienced.

As a Queer individual, you have faced adversity, but it does not diminish your worth. Your identity and value go beyond the opinions and actions of those who reject or misunderstand you. Embrace the truth: Your worth cannot be diminished by rejection. Embrace your authentic self and let go of the weight of others' judgments. Your identity is valid and beautiful, regardless of who accepts or rejects you.

I refuse to let hate diminish my spirit.

As a Queer individual, you've faced hate and discrimination, but it won't break your resilience. Know that hate does not define you; you are deserving of respect and love. Embrace this affirmation, and allow yourself to rise above negativity. Let your inner strength and pride shine, radiating positivity and inspiring others to do the same.

I deserve respect and equality.

Your worth is not defined by anyone's judgment or prejudice. Demand to be seen and heard, and never settle for anything less than the respect and equality you deserve. Embrace this reminder of the importance of advocating for your rights. Let it fuel your determination to challenge injustice, break down barriers, and create a world where every Queer person is treated with dignity and equality.

I refuse to internalize the hatred of others.

The hatred you might receive from others is not a reflection of your worth. Queer people will always have to endure hate, but refuse to let those negative thoughts and words get to you. Allow hatred to roll off your back, and continue to be the strong, beautiful, and powerful Queer individual you are.

I DESERVE TO WEAR CLOTHES THAT REFLECT WHO I AM.

My worth is not defined by sexual or romantic relationships.

Your value as a person is not conditional upon your relationship status or the approval of others. Queer people often feel like their identity is tied to their experiences, but by embracing this affirmation, you can let go of any sexual or romantic expectations. You don't have to have had any romantic or sexual encounters to know you are Queer. You are deserving of love, respect, and validation regardless of your relationship status.

The binary is a man-made idea.

The binary is a man-made concept that separates us into two groups of male and female. This idea confines us, but as a Queer individual, you know that human experiences cannot be contained by rigid categories. Embrace the freedom of existing beyond the binary. Remember that you are not limited by society's attempts to label or define you. Use this affirmation as a reminder that you are beautifully complex and can defy the limitations of the binary.

HAVING *feminine* QUALITIES DOESN'T MAKE ME LESS OF A *man.*

My asexuality is valid and real.

In a world that often centers on sexual attraction, it's essential to affirm your identity as an asexual person! Embrace the truth of your identity, knowing that it is just as valid as any other orientation. If you are asexual, write this affirmation on your mirror to remind yourself you are valid. If you don't identify as asexual, make sure to tell someone in your life who identifies as asexual about this affirmation so they feel validated!

My identity as a Queer Person of Color is beautiful.

Embrace the beauty of your intersecting identities and honor the strength that comes from navigating multiple worlds. Your journey is a testament to resilience and the richness of diversity. In a world that may seek to diminish your worth, stand proud in the truth of your existence! Your identity as a Queer Person of Color is a vibrant thread in the fabric of the Queer community.

I celebrate the intersection of my racial and Queer identities.

As a Queer individual, your racial identity is a crucial part of how you navigate your Queerness. In a world that often tries to compartmentalize and categorize, celebrate the richness that comes from the blending of your diverse experiences. Remind yourself that your intersectional identity is a source of strength and empowerment and that you have the right to celebrate every aspect of who you are.

I define my own femininity/ masculinity.

Reject societal expectations and norms, and instead, honor the unique expression of your gender identity. Whether it aligns with traditional notions or challenges them, your self-defined femininity or masculinity is beautiful and valid. You have the ability to shape and embody your gender in a way that feels true to your authentic self.

PEOPLE OF ALL GENDERS GET THEIR PERIOD.

My love for women is beautiful and valid.

Your love for women is a profound expression of your identity and a testament to the diversity of Queer love. Your love for women proves that attraction can be fluid and beautiful! Repeat this affirmation if you are a woman who loves other women or if you are bisexual/pansexual and need a reminder that your love for women is valid!

My love for men is beautiful and valid.

Your love for men transcends boundaries and challenges societal norms, reminding us all of the richness and diversity of Queer love. Repeat this affirmation if you are a man who loves other men or if you are bisexual/pansexual and need a reminder that your love for men is valid!

I embrace
expressions of

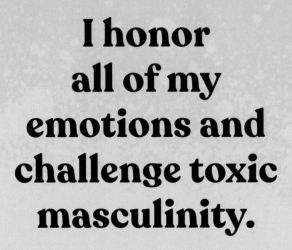

I honor all of my emotions and challenge toxic masculinity.

Challenge societal norms that dictate how you should feel, and reclaim the right to have full access to all of your emotions. Embrace vulnerability and empathy as strengths in your life, not weaknesses. Repeat this affirmation when you need a reminder to allow yourself to feel the full spectrum of human emotions despite what society says men should feel.

I am secure in my masculinity.

Know that your masculinity is not defined by rigid stereotypes. You have the power to define it yourself; be proud of that. No matter what gender you are, if you identify with aspects of masculinity, remind yourself that you can feel secure in yourself without looking to anyone else for validation.

I choose love and respect over aggression and dominance.

As a Queer person, you might be challenged by hate and discrimination, but remember that you can be the bigger person and counter with love and respect. And if you identify as a man, choosing love and respect over aggression and dominance helps you fight against toxic masculinity. Repeat this affirmation when you need a reminder to counter hate with love.

I embrace my feminine qualities.

Femininity is often seen as a weakness in our society. You get to define what femininity means to you. Don't let anyone convince you that femininity is not powerful. Allow yourself to be as feminine as you want, regardless of what society might say.

♡

i love my
transitioning
body.

My femininity does not make me inferior.

Your femininity is a strength, not a weakness. Whether you identify as a woman or just possess feminine qualities, remember that femininity is a force to be reckoned with—a source of empowerment and authenticity. Embrace the diverse expressions of femininity within you, and know that your femininity enriches the world around you and challenges outdated norms. Repeat this affirmation when you are feeling insecure about your femininity.

I challenge norms and celebrate nonconformity.

Break free from the constraints of societal norms and celebrate the beauty of nonconformity! As a Queer individual, you have the power to challenge the status quo and redefine what it means to be authentic. Embrace your uniqueness, question oppressive norms, and pave the way for a more inclusive and accepting world. Repeat this affirmation as a reminder of your courage to defy expectations and celebrate your true self.

I resist oppressive systems and advocate for liberation.

As a Queer person, it is important to recognize the urgency for change. Do your best to challenge the structures that perpetuate inequality and injustice, using your voice to uplift marginalized voices and fight for a more equitable world. Repeat this affirmation as a reminder of your power to disrupt oppressive systems and create space for liberation. Your activism and advocacy have the potential to transform lives and create lasting impact.

I honor the trailblazers who came before me.

Honor the trailblazers who paved the way for the Queer community by acknowledging their sacrifices and contributions. Admire the legacy of Queer people who came before you. They fought relentlessly for the rights and visibility you enjoy today. Let their courage and resilience inspire you to continue their fight. Repeat this affirmation as a tribute to those who came before you, recognizing their invaluable contributions in the journey toward equality.

I carry on a legacy of resilience and strength.

Remember that you are a part of a lineage of Queer individuals who have triumphed over many challenges and emerged stronger. By carrying on this legacy, you become a beacon of hope and inspiration for others, empowering them to embrace their own resilience and walk their paths with strength. Repeat this affirmation as a reminder that you are part of a bigger picture.

I honor the experiences of LGBTQIA+ elders and learn from them.

The journeys and stories of Queer elders hold invaluable lessons that can guide you on your path. Open your heart and mind to their insights, and embrace the wisdom they have to offer. Remember that you are not alone in your struggles, and there are people who have already faced similar challenges who can help. Repeat this affirmation as a reminder to listen, learn, and honor the rich tapestry of LGBTQIA+ history.

I strive to create a better future for future generations.

You hold the power to shape the future for future generations of Queer individuals. With every action and decision you make, you contribute to a world that is more inclusive and accepting. Strive to create a better future by challenging prejudice and advocating for change. Let this affirmation guide you on your path as a catalyst for progress.

I recognize the importance of preserving and sharing LGBTQIA+ history.

By recognizing the struggles, triumphs, and contributions of those who came before you, you honor their legacy and ensure that our collective history is not forgotten. Queer history is constantly neglected by society, so embrace the responsibility of preserving and sharing Queer experiences. Let this affirmation remind you of the importance of our history and inspire you to actively participate in its preservation.

I'M STILL VALID EVEN IF I'M NOT OUT.

I release comparison and embrace self-acceptance.

As a Queer individual, it's easy to fall into the trap of comparing yourself to others, whether it's your appearance, achievements, or journey. But remember, your path is unique and incomparable! Let go of the need to measure up, and instead, embrace the beauty of your authentic self. Repeat this affirmation as a reminder to stop comparing and to love yourself as you are.

I can redefine what family means.

You have the power to redefine what a family is and forge connections built on love, acceptance, and understanding. You possess the remarkable ability to build a larger, more inclusive family, one that goes beyond traditional norms and embraces the true essence of Queer love. Embrace this affirmation as a reminder that there are many types of families, and you can create one where bonds are formed by shared experiences, unconditional support, and unwavering acceptance.

I embrace the freedom to experiment and push boundaries.

Allow yourself to step outside of societal expectations and norms, discovering new aspects of your identity along the way. By pushing boundaries, you help pave the way for others to feel capable of doing the same. Repeat this affirmation as a reminder to embrace your authentic self, unapologetically and boldly.

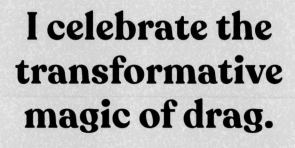

I celebrate the transformative magic of drag.

Through the power of self-expression and performance, drag allows you to explore different facets of your identity—while challenging societal norms and expectations! There is something magical about being able to transform into anything or anyone you want! Celebrate the self-love, creativity, and authenticity that comes from drag. Remember to let the magic of drag inspire you to express your true self with boldness and pride!

DRAG IS ART!

I am a loving and proud Queer parent.

You have the power to create a safe and affirming space where your children can grow, thrive, and embrace their own authentic identities. Celebrate your journey as a loving and proud Queer parent, knowing that your love and support will forever shape the lives of your children. If you are not a parent, feel free to share this affirmation with someone in your life who is!

I am proud of the positive impact I have.

Your words, actions, and presence inspire others and create ripples of change in your community. Embrace this affirmation as a reminder of the incredible influence you have and the pride you should feel for the difference you make in this world! Celebrate your ability to uplift, empower, and make a lasting impact, knowing that your existence has a positive effect on the earth.

My gender expression is valid.

There is no one way to express your gender, and your gender expression can be different from your gender identity! Society may try to impose limitations or norms, but your gender expression is valid and deserving of respect. Be proud of your journey in discovering and expressing your true self, and let this affirmation empower you to celebrate and embrace your authentic gender expression.

I don't have to fit into traditional roles.

You don't have to conform to societal expectations or fit into prescribed boxes created by society. You don't have to stick to any rules of gender or social roles. Even traditions like marriage might not speak to you, and that is completely okay! Repeat this affirmation when you feel pressured to fit into traditional gender or sexuality roles.

MY Queerness · IS · beautiful.

My Queer identity is a source of creativity and inspiration.

Your unique experiences and perspective can inspire you to be creative! Celebrate the power of your Queer identity to ignite inspiration within yourself and others. Let this affirmation be a reminder of how your Queerness can be a source of light and creative energy for you! Repeat this affirmation when you feel burned out or unmotivated.

I can be trans and nonbinary.

You challenge the limitations of gender norms and pave the way for greater understanding and acceptance by existing in both spaces. Embrace the unique intersection of your trans and nonbinary identities, celebrating the richness and diversity it brings to your life. Let this affirmation empower you to be fully seen and recognized in your identity. If this affirmation doesn't speak to you, send it to someone in your life who is trans and nonbinary to make them feel seen.

I embrace the fluidity of my attraction as a bisexual person.

Embrace the freedom to explore and connect with people across the gender spectrum, allowing yourself to fully embrace your bisexuality. Your ability to love and be attracted to different genders is a unique and powerful gift. By honoring and embracing the fluidity of your attraction, you break down barriers and challenge societal norms.

I deserve positive Queer representation.

You deserve to see yourself represented in a positive light. As a Queer individual, you have the right to demand and celebrate diverse and authentic representation in society. By acknowledging your worth and standing up for positive Queer representation, you empower yourself and others in the community. Let this affirmation remind you to advocate for visibility and inclusivity, inspiring a future where every Queer person can see themselves reflected with love and authenticity.

OUR COMMUNITY CAN UNITE AND CREATE CHANGE

I can be the representation I wish to see.

You have the power to become the representation you crave. You can be the voice, the face, and the story that inspires other Queer people! Be the proud Queer representation that you wanted to see as a young Queer kid. Empower yourself to be a positive force for change, challenging stereotypes and amplifying the diverse voices within our society.

I don't have to go through anything alone.

You have a community of support and understanding that stands with you. Remember, you don't have to face any challenge or hardship in isolation. Reach out to your chosen family, friends, or support networks who will embrace you with open arms. Together, you can navigate the complexities of life, share your triumphs and setbacks, and uplift one another. Allow yourself to lean on the strength and compassion of your Queer community.

I can always ask for help.

Seeking support is not a sign of weakness but a testament to your strength and self-awareness. Remember: You are not alone in your journey, and there are people who genuinely care and want to lend a helping hand. Whether it's seeking advice, guidance, or someone just to listen, don't hesitate to reach out. Empower yourself to prioritize your well-being and build a network of support that uplifts and validates you.

I am deserving of equal rights and opportunities.

Your sexual orientation or gender identity should not be a barrier to accessing the same rights, privileges, and opportunities that others get. Demand the equality and respect you deserve. By affirming your worth and fighting for your rights, you contribute to a more inclusive and just society where everyone can thrive. Remember, you are deserving of equal treatment, acceptance, and the freedom to live authentically without discrimination.

List of Resources

🌐 Websites/Organizations

GLAAD (www.glaad.org)

GLSEN (www.glsen.org)

It Gets Better Project (www.itgetsbetter.org)

Lambda Legal (www.lambdalegal.org)

LGBT National Help Center (www.lgbthotline.org)

National Center for Transgender Equality (www.transequality.org)

National LGBTQ Task Force (www.thetaskforce.org)

National Queer and Trans Therapists of Color Network (www.nqttcn.com)

PFLAG (www.pflag.org)

Queerty (www.queerty.com)

SAGE (www.sageusa.org)

Trans Lifeline (www.translifeline.org)

Transgender Legal Defense and Education Fund (TLDEF) (www.transgenderlegal.org)

The Trevor Project (www.thetrevorproject.org)

📖 Books

Beyond the Gender Binary by Alok Vaid-Menon

Fun Home: A Family Tragicomic by Alison Bechdel

My Queer Year: A Guided Journal by Ashley Molesso and Chess Needham

Sissy: A Coming-of-Gender Story by Jacob Tobia

Stone Butch Blues: A Novel by Leslie Feinberg

Transgender History by Susan Stryker

🎧 Podcasts

Making Gay History by Eric Marcus

Nancy by WNYC Studios (with Kathy Tu and Tobin Low)

Queer as Fact

Queery with Cameron Esposito

The Read with Kid Fury and Crissle West

Index

About the Author

Jess Vosseteig (Jess Voss Art) is a Queer illustrator and writer born and raised in Colorado. Partnering with brands and organizations like Dr. Martens, Lush, Ulta Beauty, the Ms. Foundation for Women, Facebook/Meta, and more, her work focuses on inclusivity, empowerment, and creating conversations surrounding feminism and the Queer community. Jess loves illustrating to empower all genders, break stereotypes, and promote body positivity/neutrality. Jess wants her audience to feel seen and heard in her work, and be empowered to be themselves, educate others, and push societal norms. You can find more of her work and shop at JessVossArt.com and on socials at @jessvoss_art.